The Treasure of the Tuatha Dé Danann

A pocket book of Irish Mythology

By Morgan Daimler

All Irish texts within are held in the public domain

English material copyright 2015 Morgan Daimler

ISBN-13: 978-1515210689

ISBN-10: 1515210685

Cover image, public domain, John Waterhouse "The Mystic Wood"

1914

Table of Contents

Author's Note

This pocket book represents my attempt to offer new translations of important Irish myths. Many of these stories are either difficult to find or the available translations are significantly older and often problematic. Fresh interpetations are important and offer new insight.

All the stories will be presented first in the original language, either Old or Middle Irish, followed by my translation. I have included a variety of myths which I believe are valuable, as well as a selection of miscellany which include details about the Irish Gods and pagan holidays that I think should be more widely available in English.

Táin Bó Regamna

A mbuí Cú Chuluinn i nDún Imrid gu gcúala ní an
géim. Co ndíuchrustar triana chotlad conid corustar asa
imda go riacht ind aridin ina suidiu for lár. Íar sin
immach do suidiu ar les. Cu mbu hí a ben bertho a étach
ocus a armb ina diaig. Co n-facco ní Láeg aro chinn ina
charpat inneltai oc Ferta Læig intúaig.

'Cid dot-ugai?' ol Cú Chuluinn fri Lóeg.

'Géim ro-chúalai issin maigh', ol Lóeg.

'Cid leth?' ol Cú Chuluinn.

'Aníarthúaig amne', ol Lóeg.

'Ina ndiaig', ol Cú Chuluinn.

Tíaguit ass íarum gu hÁth da Ferta. In tan mbátar ann
íarum gu gcúalatar culguiri in charpuit hi toíb Grellchui
Culguiri. Tíaguit fóe co n-faccatar ní in carpat ara cinn
no reimib. Óenech derg foa ocus óenchoss fo suidiu
ocus síthbe in charpuit sethnu ind eich co ndechuid
geinn trít fri fosad a étain anair. Bean derg hissin charpat
ocus bratt derg impi ocus di braí dergai lé ocus a brat
eter di feirt in charpuit síar co sliged lár ina diaig ocus

fer mór hi comuir in charpuit. Fúan forbbthai imme ocus gaballorg finnchuill fria aiss og immáin na bó.

'Ní fóelid in bó lib oga himmuáin', ol Cú Chuluinn.

'Ní dír duit éim a hetercert na bó so', ol in ben. 'Ní bó charat na choigcéliu duit.'

'Is dír dam-so éim baí hUlad huili', ol Cú Chuluinn.

'Eter-certar so in ba, a Chú', ol in ben.

'Ced arndid i in ben atum-gládathar?' ol Cú Chuluinn. 'Cid nach é in fer atom-gládathar?'

'In fer sin at-gládaigther-su', ol in ben.

'Ia', ol Cú Chuluinn, 'ol is tusso ara-labrathar.'

'hÚargóeth sceo lúachuir sgeo. . .ainm in fir sin', olsí.

'Amae, is amru fot in anmu', ol Cú Chului nn. 'Ba tusa trá atom glátathar in fecht so ol nim acalladar in fer. Cía do chomainm-siu féin?' ol Cú Chuluinn.

'Ní ansa. In ben sin at-gládaither-su', ol in fer, 'fóebar beo béoil, coim diúir, foltt sgeanb, gairitt sgeo úath hí a hainm', olse.

'Meraigi do-gníth-siu dim-so', ol Cú Chuluinn, 'fon innus sin.'

4

Lingid Cú Chuluinn la soduin issin charpat ocus forrumai a da chois fora dib glúinib-siu ocus a chleitíni fora mullach.

'Na himbir imrinniu éim formb', ol Cú Chuluinn.

'Scuith dim didiu', olsi. 'Am bancháinti-siu ém', olsí, 'ocus is ó Dáiriu mac Fiachno a cCúailgniu tuccus in mbuin si a ndúais n-airchetail.'

'Cluinium th'airchetal didiu', ol Cú Chuluinn.

'Scuith dim nammá', ol in ben. 'Ní ferdo duitt amin na chrothai húas mo chinn', olsí.

Tét didiu Cú Chuluinn íarum co mbuí eter di feirt in charpuit.

Gaibid-se in laíd si: Doermais nomgaib gaib eti eblatar tairichta muirtemniu morochrat romlec dianedim fiach amainsi nachach toarbair adomling airddhe oenmairb maige sainb croí chengach cocbith mestinglinne let leiss finn frithoiss dobeoib brectith reth tuasailg osdum arai airdd cechlastair cuailngne achuchuluinn... ...arindlindsi arsoegaul de antuaith .i. cluas indairmgretha.

Fo-ceird Cú Chuluinn bedg ina charpat feissin íarum. Naicc ní i nneoch íarum in mnaí nach in carpat nach in

n-ech nach in fer nach in mbuin ocus co n-faco-sium
íarum ba hén-si dub forsin chroíb ina farrud.

'Doltach ben atat-chomnaic', ol Cú Chuluinn.

'Is Dollud dono bias forsinn greallaig si co bráth', ol
in ben. Grellach Dolluid íarum a hainm ó hoin ille.

'Ochti ro-feisind bed tú ní samluid no-scarfamais', ol
Cú Chuluinn.

'Cid donrignis', olsí, 'bieith olec de.'

'Ni chumgai olc dam', ol Cú Chuluinn.

'Cumgaim écin', olsin ben. 'Is oc do ditin do báis-siu
atáu-so ocus bia', ollsí. 'Do-ucus-sa in mboin si éim',
olsí, 'a síd Crúachan condo rodart in Donn Cúailgni lem
.i. tarb Dáre maic Fiachnui ocus is é aret bia-so i mbetho
gu rab dartaid in lóeg fil ina bruinn ina bó so ocus is hé
consaídfe Táin Bé Cúailgni.'

'Bíam airdirciu-sa di din Táin hí sin', ol Cú
Chuluinn.

''Géna a n-ánrado.

Brisfe a mérchatho.

Bia tigba na Táno.''

'Cinnus con-igfa-sa anní sin', ol in ben. 'Ar in tain
no-mbia-sa oc comrac fri fer comthrén comchroda

comchliss comfobaith coméscaith comchiníuil comgaiscid comméti friut .i. bam esccung-so ocus fo-chichiur curu immot chossa issinn áth gu mba héccomlunn mór.'

'For-tonga do día tuingthe Ulaid', ol Cú Chuluinn, 'fortat-naesab- su fri glaisslecta ind átho ocus nicot bia ícc húaim-siu de gu bráth manim derguis-so.'

'Bia sod-sa dono glass duit-si', olsí, 'ocus géba bréit dot dóidind deiss conicci do rigid clí.'

'Tongu-sa do día tuingti hUlaid', ol Cú Chuluinn, 'not-benabsi secham gom chletíne gu mbeba do súil it chinn ocus nocot bia ícc húaim-siu de go bráth manim dergais-si.'

'Biam samuiscc-siu finn áuoderg dono', olsissiu, 'ocus do-rag issinn linn hi fail inn áthu in n-atan ro-mbia-so oc comrucc fri fer buss choimchliss duitt ocus cét noud finn n-óbrecc imm diaig ocus membuis inn ét huili im diaig-siu issin n-áth ocus con-bibustar fír fer fort-so a llaa sin ocus géttair do chenn ditt issinn áth sin.'

'Tungu et reliqua, fo-chichiur-sa hurchur asmo thábaill fortt- sa co memba do gerr gara foat ocus nico

mbia ícc húaim-si de co bráth manim dergais-si ocus
nicom géntar-so a llá sin etir', ol Cú Chuluinn.

Scarsait íar sin ocus luid Cú Chuluinn for cúlo
dorithisiu do Dún Imrith ocus luithi in Morrígan cona
buin hi síd Crúachan la Connachta.

Stokes, W., (1880). Irische Texte mit Übersetzugen
und Wörterbuch

The Cattle Raid of Regamna

When Cu Chulain was in Dun Imrid he heard something; it was the roaring of cattle. So that he woke up and was thrown out of bed and reached the bench that was sitting on the floor. After that he went outside into the yard. And it was his wife, following behind him, who brought his clothing and his armor. And he saw something in front of him, Laeg in his chariot, harnessed at Ferta Laeg in the north.

"What brings you?" said Cu Chulain to Laeg.

"The roaring of cattle that I heard in the field," said Laeg.

"What direction?" said Cu Chulain.

"In the north-west, thus," said Laeg.

"Follow on them," said Cu Chulain.

After this they went out to Ath de Ferta. After, while they were there, they heard a noise of the chariot in the side of Grellach Culgairi. They went down and saw a chariot before them. One red horse with a single leg was pulling it, and the shaft of the chariot went through the horse to the front of it's forehead. A red-haired woman with red eyebrows was in the chariot with a red cloak around her shoulders; the cloak hung down at the back of the chariot and dragged on the ground behind her. There was a big man in front of the chariot wearing a tunic carrying a forked white hazel stick that he used to drive the cow.

"The cow is not pleased with her driving," said Cu Chulain.

"Indeed it is not necessary to you to judge this cow," said the woman. "It is not a friend's nor a companion's cow to you."

"Indeed, the cows of all the Ulstermen are necessary to me," said Cu Chulain

"You decide much, oh, Cu Chulain," said the woman.

"Why is it that the woman speaks to me?" said Cu Chulain. "Why not him, the man, who speaks to me?"

"It's not the man that you shouted to", said the woman.

"Ha!", said Cu Chulain, "Speak and you speak in his voice."

"Cold wind-conflict-brightness-strife is his name" she said

"Indeed, that name is wonderful throughout", said Cu Chulain. "Then you are bound to speaking the course of this conversation for the man. What do you name yourself?" said Cu Chulain.

"Not difficult. The woman who you are speaking to," said the man, "is Keen edged-small lipped-plain cloaked-hair-sharp shouting-fierceness-a phantom."

"You give me an idiot's counsel"[1], said Cu Chulain, "based in this."

Cu Chulain jumped beside her in the chariot and set his two feet on her knees and his dart[2] against the crown of her head.

"Who puts this point indeed?" said Cu Chulain.

"A small something then", said she.

"I am a woman satirist indeed", said she, "and it is from Dáire mac Fiachnai of Cuilgne that I bring the cow; she is a poet's reward for a poem"'

---

[1] this may be better relayed in English as "You must think I'm an idiot to tell me this" ie he thinks they are intentionally playing with him.

[2] literally cleittíne a small dart or javelin which was one of Cu Chulain's particular weapons.

"I'll hear the poem then", said Cu Chulain.

"A small something only", said the woman. "Not manly to you thus while brandishing over my head", said she.

Then after Cu Chulain went so that he was between the two poles of the chariot.

She gave this poem[3]:

"Low-born-foundation you grab,

Take a herd driven,

Eastward-blown Muirrthemne,

Great misery, chief stone, hurrier,

Raven fierce but not

Bringing great floods

Peak of fame unique death

Plain of Sainb heart, every head

World-warring judgment

Half a glen severed

Bright wild place, your life

Deceitful arrival runs

---

[3] The majority of the Irish material here is from the Yellow Book of Lecan version, however the Morrigan's satire poem is the von Egerton version, both found in Windisch's Irische Texte mit Ubersetzugen and Worterbuchen

Over poet's-demands
Over mound's messenger
Your direction, every burning
Cuailigne, oh Cu Chulainn.."

Cuchulain sprang onto his own chariot after that. Then nothing was there of all of them not the woman, not the chariot, not the horse, not the man, not the cow and he saw that she was a black bird on a branch near him.

"A hurtful woman you are," said Cuchulain.

"It is Dollud [distress] then that will be on this bog until Doomsday," said the woman. Bog of Distress was its name from that time afterwards.

"If only I had known it was you," said Cuchulain, "not this way would we have separated."

"Whatever you would have done," said she, "misfortune would result from it."

"You cannot bring misfortune to me," said Cuchulain.

"I am able indeed," said the woman; "It is bringing about your death I am and shall be," said she.

"I brought this cow then," she said, "from the fairy mound of Cruachan so that she was mounted by the Brown Bull of Cuilgne by me, that is the bull of Daire mac Fiachnai. And it is that interval you be in life, until the calf in the womb of this cow is a young bull, and it is this that stirs up the cattle raid of Cuilgne."

"I will be renowned through this aforementioned cattle raid," said Cu Chulain. "I will kill their champions. Defeat their big battles. I will survive the cattle raid."

"How will you do this aforementioned?" said the woman. "For at the time of your combat with a man of similar strength, similar form, similar skill, similar quickness, similar alertness, similar tribe, similar weapons, similar greatness, against you I will be an eel throwing twists about your feet in the ford until it will be greatly unfair odds."

"I swear to a God Ulstermen swear to," said Cu Chulain, "I will kick you against blue-grey[4] stones of the

---

[4] for those who are interested in the use of color in Irish material its given here as glas, or green, but green which can be anything from a light green or blue to a blue grey.

ford and there will be no cure for you from me for it until Doomsday if you don't ask my forgiveness."

"I will be a blue-grey[5] wolf-bitch then against you," she said. "And I will take a strip from your wrist on the right up to your forearm on the left."

"I swear to a God Ulstermen swear to," said Cu Chulain,"I will wound you myself with my dart until your eye bursts in your head and there will be no cure for you from me for it until Doomsday if you don't ask my forgiveness."

"I will be a red-eared white heifer then," said she, "and I will come in the water in a place of the ford another time you will be at combat with a man as skilled as you and a hundred red-eared white cows after me; all the cows behind me will burst into the ford and violate fair combat[6] against you. And your head will be taken away off you in that very ford."

"I will swear by others, I will throw a cast out of my sling at you- and with it break the lower part of your leg

---

[5] See previous footnote for discussion of use of "green" to mean blue-grey

[6] In Old Irish "fir fer" literally "men's truth". This concept is the bases of honorable combat in Irish warfare and hinges on the idea of one-on-one fighting of equal opponents.

shortly and by no means will there be a cure for you from me for it until Doomsday if you don't ask my forgiveness and that will not be done any day at all', said Cu Chulain.

They separated and Cu Chulain went back along his course to Dún Imrith and the Morrigan went with the cow to the fairy hill of Cruachan in Connacht.

The Morrigan's Satire Poem

I thought it would be interesting to show you the differences between the two versions of the Morrigan's satire poem which appear in the Táin Bó Regamna. I'll give theYellow Book of Lecan version first followed by the von Egerton version, both found in the Irische Texte mit Übersetzugen und Wörterbuch:

Doernais namgaib

Gaib eiti ablatutar

ie n Muirrthemne

(daruber .i. arg mag Murthemne).

Moracrat romleic diamaigi

fiachanma amanse

nach cach do arbiur

adomlig.

Ardbae aen marb

maigi Sainb (daruber .i. Ai)

Cerda croichengach

cochbith metsin glinni

lat les find fir itho is de

buaib brethai treth

tuasailc os do marai

airdde cechlastar

Cnailngi a Cuculainn fri

burach mbuaid ar

cuailgi a Cuchulainn cair.

Buidi ben basa claen

cuil arm deisi ar saegal

dian taith .i. cluas armgreta.

Slave-bound you grab

Take a herd driven

Gifts of Muirrthemne

(that is noble plain of Muirrthemne)

Great misery, chief stone, mighty lamentation,

Fierce ravens

Not each to you brings

Great fearsome glory.

High-profit a unique death

the plain of Sainb (that is Ai)

Skilled each-skin

World-warring judgment glens

Half severed, bright men hunger and you

arrogant decide a herd

Above demands and your existence

Your direction, every burning

Cuiligne, oh Cu Chulainn, towards

Furious victory from

Cuiligne, oh guilty Cu Chulainn.

Gratitude a woman unjust death

Violating weapon, hosts against a lifetime

True binding, that is hear weapons-strikes

The alternate von Egerton version is:

Doermais nomgaib

gaib eti eblatar

tairichta muirtemniu

morochrat romlec dianedim

fiach amainsi nachach

toarbair adomling

airddhe oenmairb

maige sainb croí chengach

cocbith mestin-

glinne let leiss

finn frithoiss dobeoib

brectith reth

tuasailg osdum arai

airdd cechlastair

cuailngne achuchuluinn.

"Low-born-foundation you grab,

Take a herd driven,

Eastward-blown Muirrthemne,

Great misery, chief stone, hurrier,

Raven fierce but not

Bringing great floods

Peak of fame unique death

Plain of Sainb heart, every head

World-warring judgment

Half a glen severed

Bright wild place, your life

Deceitful arrival runs

Over poet's-demands

Over mound's messenger

Your direction, every burning

Cuilnge, oh Cu Chulain..."

De Gabail In tSide

Boí rí amra for Tuathaib Dea i nHere. Dagan a ainm.
Ba mór dí a chumachta, ced la Maccu Miled iar ngabail
in tíre. Ar collset Tuatha Dea ith ocus blicht im Maccu
Miled. Co ndingsat chairddes in Dagdai. Doessartsaide
iarum ith ocus blicht dóib. Ba mór dí a chumachtasom in
tan ba rí i tossuch, ocus ba hé fodail inna side do feraib
Dea .i. Lug mac Ethnend i sSíd Rodrubán, Ogma i sSíd
Aircheltrai, Don Dagdu fessin im Síth Leithet
Lachtmaige oí asíd Cnocc Báine. Brú Ruair. Síd in
Broga dano ba laiss i tossuch, amal asberat. Do lluid dí
in Mac Oac cosin Dagda, do chungid feraind o forodail
do chách, ba daltasaide dí do Midir Breg Léith, ocus do
Nindid fáith,

"Nimthá duit" ol in Dagda. "Ni tharnaic fodail
lemm."

"Etá dam dí" ol in Mac Ooc. "Cid bia co n-aidchi it
trib féin. "dobreth dosom ón iarum.

"Collá dot daim tra" ol in Dagda

"uaire doromailt do ré Is menand" olse. "is laa ocus
adaig in bith uile. Ocus iss ed on doratad damsa."

Luid dó Dagán ass iarum ocus anaid in Macc Oóc ina síd. Amra dano a tír hisin. Ataat tri chrand co torud and do grés, ocus mucc bithbeo fo chossaib ocus mucc fonaithe. Ocus lestar co llind sainemail. Ocus ni erchranand sin uile do grés.

- Lebar na Núachongbála, (n.d.)

The Taking of the Sí

There was a marvelous king of the Tuatha Dea in Ireland. Dagda was his name. Great was his power, even in the present time when the Sons of Mil have taken the land, on account of the Tuatha Dea destroying the grain and milk of the Sons of Mil, until they made an alliance with the Dagda. Afterwards he preserves the grain and milk for them.

Great was his power while he was king in the beginning and he distributed the sí to the men of the Gods that is Lug mac Ethne in the sí at Rodrubán, Ogma in the sí at Aircheltra, the Dagda himself the sí Leithet Lachtmaige, sheep-ful the White Mound, Brú Ruair. The sí of Broga then was among his at the beginning, as they say. Then the Mac Oc went to Dagda seeking territory but it was all dispersed; he was a fosterson to Midir Breg Leith and Nindid the Seer.

"There is nothing to go to you", said the Dagda. "Everything has been distributed by me."

"Obtain for me this," said the Mac Oc, "even hospitality with the following night in your own place." This was given to him afterwards.

"Your time as a guest is over[7]," said the Dagda.

"Hours consume a man's time, it is evident," he said."It is a day and night in life always. And it is the aforementioned I was given."

The Dagda went out afterwards and the Mac Oc remained in the sí. Wonderful moreover his land there. There were three trees with produce there on them always, and a pig always in life on its feet, and a pig roasted. And a vessel with distinctive drink. And all these things never fail, always.

---

[7] * This is a bit awkward to render in English. Literally it's "Spent is your legitimate guest to you then"

Berba

Berba, canas ro ainmniged?

Ni ansa. Meiche mac na Morrigna is and robatar na tri crideda, corot-marb Mac cecht im-Maig Mechi. Mag Fertaigi dano a ainm in maige co sin. Amlaidh badar na cride sin, co ndelbaib tri nathrach treithib. Meni torsed dano bas do Mechi arforbertais na nathracha ind & focnafed ana faigbet béo i nHérinn. Roloisc iarum Mac cecht inna cride sin im-Maig Luathat, coro la al-luaith lasin sruth, conid romarb eas in tsrotha, ocuscoro marb cach n-anmanda roboi ann, ocus coro mberb. Nó combad i n-Aird Luaithrid noloisc. Unde Berba dicitur ocus Mag Meche ocus Aird Luaithrid. Nó comad Berba .i. ber nó bir ocus ba .i. balb. Unde Berba dicitur .i. usce balb.

- Stokes, W., (1894). The Prose Tales of the Rennes Dindshenchas

Berba – The story of the Morrigan's Son

Berba, why this name?

Not difficult. Meiche was a son of the Morrigan and he had three hearts, until he was killed by Mac Cecht at Maige Mechi. Maige Fertaigi was the name of the plain before that. This way were those hearts, with three forms of three serpents. Moreover if not for the death of Meiche, the serpents would have grown to the end and consumed therefore all life in Ireland. Then Mac Cecht burned the hearts there at Maig Luathat, throwing the ashes in the course of the river, so that the rapids in the stream died, and brought death to every animal there and boiling. Or else he may have destroyed them in Ard Luaithard (or he burned them). So Berba is said and Mag Meche and Ard Luauthrid.

Or it's called Berba, that is ber or bir – water – and ba that is balb – silent – whence Berba is called silent water.

An Dindshenchas de Emain Macha

Cid diatá Eomuin Machae? Ni hanse. Bui righi n-
Erenn hi comflaithius etir Ruad mac m-Bodhuirn &
Cimbaeth mac Finntain & Dithorbae mac Dimain. Secht
m-bliedna do cech oe hi flaith h-Erenn. Imcloeth beus hi
cinn hsecht m-bliada na. Ocus is amlaid do-faspenta a
righe do flaith nod-gebed beus: 'Ind flaith si do-
asselbtur duit a taspenad uait a n-ógi .i. dom-biur duit
cen gái cen ethech cen imarbae cen anfir flatha. Glinne
aurut friss .i. secht n-octhigerna & secht righ (no druith)
& secht file .i. na h-oigthigirn dot fognam, na druith dot
ressadh & dott imdergadh, na filid dott aorad tre m-
bricht co rabuit i talmain ria nomaide'. Is amlaid sin tra
do-aissilbith ind flaith co m-betiss immurgu na torthae
iarna coir lasna flaithi. Is aire dognidiss in sin.

Marb iar suidhiu Dithorba mac Demain, co n-gabsat a
mec a forba flatha .i. Baeth & Brass & Betach & Uallach
& Borbchass coic maic Dithorbai maic Demain. Do-
rochair lobra dano for Ruad mac m-Boduirn, diata Ess
Ruaid isin tuaiscert. Ni farcuib side cloinn inge
aoninginnamma. Macha a h-ainm-sidhe. O ssniastar side

in flaith {MS page 69} a comarbus a h-athar nissnarroet Cimbaeth i comflaithius. 'Do-ber-sa dam-sa illau catha', ol sissi. Do-gnither son & feguir cath eturru & memaid for Cimbaeth. Gebaid si in flaith co cend secht m-bliadan. Tanic do Chimbaeth aimserá na flatha.

'Ni bera', ol in ingen, 'conidruca ar ecin'.

Fechuir cadh ann eturrua. Memaid for Cimbaeth. Geabuid si danoflaithius co cenn secht m-bliadan. Tanic co maccuib Dithorbae in sel flatha. Feruid si cadh friu. Maidid rempe-si. Do meil si dano flaithius Dithorbai. Luid Cimbaeth cuice-si co m-bu he a fer & gaibid sí righi n-Erenn. Lottar maic Dithorbae for fogail & ba trom in chaladfhogal. Cech mac uilc robai ind-Eire do-choid chuca. In baile hi fuacartais nofhoglatiss ann. Ro-hearbad dano h-uadi-si naonbur cech tuaithe for a n-iarair ocus do rimarta geill cecha feine di-si dar cenn na n-drochmac batar forsan b-fogail. Con-dahualgnigset a feine ar a tuidecht dia m-bailib, co na rabadar maic Dithorbai acht a n-aonur .i. a coic. Maoite a fogal-sum anacumauc asennud. Luid si iarum feisin for a n-iarair indhi Macha a h-aonar ocus facbais Cimbaeth ina suidiu & indleatha taos secuil impi-si & ceirt impi & ballan

mor ina laim & lauidi fo h-Erinn for a n-iarir, co ro-
tuarascfat adi i m-Buirind Connacht. Al-luide ina n-diaid
isin dithrub con[...] arnic iman tenid. Suidid accu ocon
tene & at-luidestar comruc friu nacha teostaiss co in a h-
aenur.

'Can do-dechad, a banscal?' ol in oig.

'Is do cein & fhogus on', ol sisi.

Do-berat biad di & doim-gairett dul chuice.

'Nato', ol sisi. 'Caillech amnachtach truagh, ni coir
mu t-saurugad.'

'Con-ricfa fri firu anocht, a chaillech', ol seat. 'Cia
raghas chuice a tosaig?'

'Misi', ol in sindsir .i. ol Baeth. Luid side focetoir.
Do-bert a sliasait dar a braguit.

'Fe amai!' ol se, 'marb amin ben ocaib.'

'At fer trogh', ol Brass. Luid side don cennu. Do-ber
si dano a cois tar suide. Ticc a ceile. Fo-rurmed [...]
dano. Tecuit uile & at-raig forru & ataig lomain forra .i.
[...] uile ocus imatacht reimpi co rainic Eamuin [...] dia
marbad.

'Nato', ol sisi. 'Oc saighid a cirt robatar. Is anbfir a marbad. Do-berthar immurgu fo daoire di foghnum dam-sa.'

'Cissi daoire do-berthar forru? Is anfir a [...] daorad [...]

'Is fior', ol si. 'Claidid dano in raith immácuairt.' Suidid forro & eo gairid ina laim & do fóruinn impi toraind na ratha & ro cechladar maic Dithorba inn raith .i. int eo argait ro boi do-rat dar a muin oc torainn na ratha. Conid de sin ata Eamuin Macha inghine Ruaidhi & rl. Finit.

- Meyer, K., (1907) Archiv für Celtische Lexikographie

The Story of the Name of Emain Macha

Why the name of Emhain Macha? Not difficult. There were kings in Ireland who shared the sovereignty between them: Ruad mac m-Bodhuirn and Cimbaeth mac Finntain and Dithorbae mac Dimain. Seven years to each one ruling Ireland. Well-known to this day that division of seven years. And it is thus a king announces he possesses his sovereignty: "The point of his sovereignty assigned a few requirements of his perfection, that is judging to you without lying, without perjury, without deceit, without unjust sovereignty. A security with them against him that is seven young lords and seven kings (or druids) and seven poets, that is the the young lords to be in servitude, the druids to satirize him and to embarrass him, the poets to insult his battle prowess so that he is in earth before a period of nine days and nights". It is thus that it is throughout the parts of the world concerning sovereignty, later they are struck with correct sovereignty. A nobleman's making is in that.

Then Dithorba mac Demain died, with his sons to take the completion of his sovereignty that is Baeth and Brass and Betach and Uallach and Borbchass the five sons of Dithorbai maic Demain. A sickness fell besides upon Ruad mac m-Boduirn, named Ess Ruaid in the north. Beside him consequently his family was a daughter, his only child. Macha was her name. She rose up therefore in sovereignty in succession of her father; unwilling was Cimbaeth to be in shared sovereignty.

"I will give battle", said she.

They make a return and fierce battle between them and Cimbaeth flees. She was then in sovereignty for seven years. After this time the sovereignty was to go to Cimbaeth.

"It was not appointed", said the maiden, "but granted in the compulsion of battle".

Fierce battle there between them; defeat for Cimbaeth. She captures then his sovereignty period of seven years. The sovereignty went with the sons of Dithorbae in turn. She supplies battle against them. They flee before her. She then consumes the sovereignty of Dithorbai. Cimbaeth goes towards her with his possessions [and becomes] her husband and she takes possession of the rulership of Ireland.

The sons of Dithorbae go to raiding and hard living in a raiding-place. Each unlucky son who is in Ireland goes hence. They proclaim a settlement there. They trust no one as all people are seeking them and counting pledges against them from her and on behalf of the bad sons who are pillaging. In their pride they themselves battle when arriving in their own land where they are sons of Dithorbai, but they are alone and in secret. Their goods were wretched plunder in the end.

She goes afterwards herself searching for them; Macha, she alone, leaving Cimbaeth established she divides rye dough about herself and rags about her and great blemishes on her hands and sets out across Ireland seeking them. Beginning in the north-west for that reason in the region of Connacht. She went after that to a wilderness with [...] she finds their fire. They were in that place with a fire and move to fight any who have gone there alone.

"What brings you, oh woman?" said the youths.

"I'm always without and in injured disgrace", said she. They give food to her and laugh, going towards her.

"By no means", said she. "A foolish, wretched old woman, it's not proper for you to violate me."

"Join with us against your fulfillment[8] tonight, oh old woman", said he. "Who will choose to begin with her?"

"Me", said the eldest, that is said Baeth. She goes freely. She brings him as a hostage with her two thighs.

"Woe, alas" said he, "deadly thus an exalted woman."

"I'll go after the embarrassed man", said Brass. She goes to the place apart. Takes she then the feet of the aforementioned. He becomes her servant. For [...] then. She goes to each and overcomes them and impels ropes on them that is [...] each and binds in ropes until they reach Eamuin [...] for the purpose of killing.

"By no means", said she. "is this advancing correctness. Their killing would be an injustice. Bring them together under unfreeness from service to me."

---

[8] *the implication here is that because they fed her a meal she owes them a forfeit, hence firu, "righteousness, truth" is given here as fulfillment although it could be read as well as "join with us against your righteousness"; the idea remains the same either way.

"How long will unfreeness be carried on them? It's an injustice his [...] servitude [...]

'It's a surety" said she. "They will dig then the circumference trench of the fort"

She arranges them and calls her brooch to her hand and to the rocks about her outlines the fort and gives tidings to the sons of Dithorba of the fort, that is the silver brooch given, me thinks, from her neck which outlined the fort. Thus is it Eamuin Macha for the daughter of Ruaidhi. The end.

Aislinge Oenguso

Boí Óengus in n-aidchi n-aili inna chotlud. Co n-accae ní, in n-ingin cucci for crunn síuil dó. Is sí as áilldem ro boí i n-Ére. Luid Óengus do gabáil a l-lámae dia tabairt cucci inna imdai. Co n-accae ní; fo-sceinn úad opunn. Nícon fitir cia árluid h-úad. Boí and co arabárach. Nípo slán laiss a menmae. Do-génai galar n-dó in delb ad-condairc cen a h-accaldaim. Nícon luid biad inna béolu. Boí and do aidchi dano aithirriuch. Co n-accae timpán inna láim as bindem boíe. Sennid céol n-dó. Con-tuil friss. Bíid and co arabárach. Nícon ro-proindig dano arabárach.

Blíadain lán dó os sí occa aithigid fon séol sin condid corastar i sergg. Nícon epert fri nech. F-a-ceird i sergg íarum ocus ní fitir nech cid ro m-boí. Do-ecmalldar legi Érenn. Nícon fetatar-som cid ro m-boí asendud. Ethae co Fíngen, liaig Conchobuir. Do-tét-side cucci. Ad-gninad-som i n-aigid in duini a n-galar no bíth for ocus ad-gninad din dieid no théiged din tig a l-lín no bíth co n-galar and.

Atn-gládastar for leith.

"Ate! nítat béodai do imthechta", ol Fíngen, "Sercc écmaise ro carais."

"Ad-rumadar mo galar form", ol Óengus.

"Do-rochar i n-dochraidi ocus ní rolámar a epirt fri nech", ol Fíngen.

"Is fír deit", ol Óengus. "Do-m-ánaic ingen álaind in chrotha as áilldem i n-Ére co n-écusc derscaigthiu. Timpán inna l-láim, conid senned dam cach n-aidchi."

"Ní báe", ol Fíngen, "do-rogad duit cairdes frie; ocus foítter úait cossin m-Boinn, cot máthair, co tuidich dot accaldaim."

Tíagair cuicce. Tic iarum in Boann. "Bíu oc frepaid ind fir-se", ol Fíngen, "d-an-ánaic galar n-ainchis".

Ad-fíadot a scéla don Boinn.

"Bíd a freccor céill dia máthair", ol Fíngen. "D-an-ánaic galar n-ainchis; ocus timchelltar h-úait Ériu uile, dús in n-étar h-úait ingen in chrotha so ad-condairc do macc".

Bíid oc suidiu co cenn m-blíadnae. Nícon frith ní ba chosmail di. Is iar sin con-gairther Fíngen doib aithirriuch.

"Nícon frith cobair isindísiu", ol Boann.

As-bert Fíngen: "Foítter cossin n-Dagdae tuidecht do accaldaim a maicc".

Tíagair cossin n-Dagdae. Ticc-side aithirriuch. "Cid diandom-chomgrad?'"

"Do airli do maicc", ol in Boann. "Is ferr duit a chobair. Is liach a dul immudu. At-tá i siurgg. Ro car seircc écmaise ocus ní roachar a chobair".

"Cia torbae mo accaldam?" ol inDagdae. "Ní móo mo éolas in- dáthe-si".

"Móo écin", ol Fíngen. "Is tú rí síde n-Érenn; ocus tíagar úaib co Bodb, ríg síde Muman, ocus is deilm a éolas la h-Érinn n-uili".

Ethae co suide. Feraid-side fáilti friu. "Fo chen dúib", ol Bodb, "a muinter in Dagdai".

"Is ed do-roachtmar".

"Scéla lib?" ol Bodb.

"Atáat linni: Óengus macc in Dagdai i siurgg dá blíadnae."

"Cid táas?" ol Bodb.

"Ad-condairc ingin inna chotlud. Nícon fetammar i n-Ére cia h-airm i tá ind ingen ro char ocus ad-condairc.

Timmarnad duit ón Dagdae co comtastar h-úait fond Érinn ingen in chrotha-sa ocus ind écuisc."

"Con- díastar", ol Bodb, "ocus étar dál blíadnae friumm co fessur fis scél".

Do-lluid cinn blíadnae co tech m-Buidb co Síd Ar Femen.

"To-imchiullus Érinn n-uili co fuar in n-ingen oc Loch Bél Dracon oc Crottaib Cliach", ol Bodb.

Tíagair úaidib dochum in Dagdai. Ferthair fáilte friu. "Scéla lib?" ol in Dagdae.

"Scéla maithi; fo-fríth ind ingen in chrotha-so asrubartaid. Timmarnad duit ó Bodb. Táet ass Óengus linni a dochum dús in n-aithgne in n-ingin, conda accathar."

Brethae Óengus i carput co m-boí oc Síd Al Femen. Fled mór lassin ríg ara ciunn. Ferthae fáilte friss. Bátar trí láa ocus teora aidchi ocond fleid.

"Tair ass trá", ol Bodb, "dús in n-aithgne in n-ingin conda aiccther."

"Ci ad-da-gnoe, ní-s cumcaim-si a tabairt acht ad-nda-cether namá."

To-lotar íarum co m-bátar oc Loch. Co n-accatar inna tri cóecta ingen macdacht. Co n-accatar in n-ingin n-etarru. Ní tacmuictis inna h-ingena dí acht coticci a gualainn. Slabrad airgdide eter cach dí ingin. Muince airgdide imma brágait fadisin ocus slabrad di ór forloiscthiu. Is and as-bert Bodb: "In n-aithgén in n-ingen n-ucut?"

"Aithgén écin", olÓengus.

"Ní-m thá-sa cumacc deit", ol Bodb, "bas móo."

"Ní báe són", ol Óengus, "ém; óre as sí ad-condarc; ní cumcub a breith in fecht-so.Cuich ind ingen-sa, a Buidb?" ol Óengus.

"Ro-fetar écin", ol in Bodb, "Caer Ibormeith, ingen Ethail Anbuail a s-Síd Úamain i crích Connacht".

Do-comlat ass íarum Óengus ocus a muinter dochum a críche. Téit Bodb laiss co n-árlastar in n-Dagdae ocus in m-Boinn oc Bruig Maicc ind Óicc. Ad-fíadat a scéla doib ad-fídatar doib amail m-boíe eter cruth ocus écoscc amail ad-condarcatar. Ocus ad-fídatar a h-ainm ocus ainm a h-athar ocus a senathar.

"Ní ségdae dúnn", ol in Dagdae, "ná cumcem do socht."

"Aní bad maith duit, a Dagdai", olBodb. "Eircc dochum n-Ailella ocus Medbae ar is leo bíid inna cóiciud ind ingen."

Téit in Dagdae co m-boí i tírib Connacht, trí fichit carpat a lín. Ferthae fáilte friu lassin ríg ocus in rígnai. Bátar sechtmain láin oc fledugud íar sin im chormann doib. "Cid immu-b-rácht?" ol in rí.

"At-tá ingen lat-su it ferunn'", ol in Dagdae, "ocus ro-s car mo macc-sa, ocus do-rónad galar dó. Do-dechad-sa cuccuib dús in-da-tartaid don macc."

"Cuich?" ol Ailill.

"Ingen Ethail Anbuail."

"Ní linni a cumacc", ol Ailill ocus Medb. "Dia cuimsimmis do-bérthae dó."

"Ani for-maith -congairther rí in t-síde cuccuib", ol in Dagdae.

Téit rechtaire Ailella cucci. "Timmarnad duit ó Ailill ocus Meidb dul dia n-accaldaim".

"Ní reg-sa", ol sé. "Ní tibér mo ingin do macc in Dagdai". Fásagar co h-Ailill anísin. "Ní étar fair a thuidecht; ro-fitir aní dia con-garar."

"Ní báe', ol Ailill, "do-rega-som ocus do-bértar cenna a laech laiss."

Íar sin cot-éirig teglach n-Ailella ocus muinter in Dagdai dochum in t-síde. Inrethat a síd n-uile. Do-smberattrí fichtea cenn ass ocus in ríg co m-boí i Crúachnaib i n-ergabáil.

Is íarum as-bert Ailill fri h-Ethal n-Anbuail: "tabair do ingin do macc in Dagdai."

"Ni cumcaim", ol sé. "Is móo a cumachtae in- dó."

"Ced cumachtae mór fil lee?" ol Ailill.

"Ní anse; bíid i n-deilb éuin cach la blíadnai, in m-blíadnai n-aili i n-deilb duini."

"Ci-ssí blíadain m-bís i n-deilb éuin?" ol Ailill.

"Ní lemm-sa a mrath", ol a h-athair.

"Do chenn dít", ol Ailill, "mani-n-écis-ni."

"Níba sia cucci dam-sa", ol sé.

"At-bérsa", ol sé; "is lérithir sin ro-n gabsaid occai. In t-samuin-se as nessam bieid i n-deilb éuin oc Loch Bél Dracon, ocus ad-cichsiter sain-éuin lee and, ocus bieit trí cóecait géise n-impe; ocus at-tá aurgnam lemm-sa doib."

"Ni báe lemm-sa iarum," ol in Dagdae, "óre ro-fetar a h-aicned do-s-uc-so".

Do-gníther íarum cairdes leu .i. Ailill ocus Ethal ocus in Dagdae ocus soírthair Ethal ass. Celebraid in Dagdae doib. Ticc in Dagdae dia thig ocus ad-fét a scéla dia macc. "Eirc immon samuin as nessam co Loch Bél Dracon con-da-garae cuccut dind loch".

Téit in Macc Óc co m-boí oc Loch Bél Dracon. Co n-accae trí cóecta én find forsind loch cona slabradaib airgdidib co caírchesaib órdaib imma cenna. Boí Óengus i n-deilb doínachta for brú ind locha. Con-gair in n-ingin cucci. "Tair dom accaldaim, a Chaer."

"Cia do-m-gair?" ol Caer. "Cotot-gair Óengus."

"Regait diandom fhoíme ar th' inchaib co tís a l-loch mofhrithisi."

"Fo-t-sisiur", ol sé.

Téiti cucci. Fo-ceird-sium dí láim forrae. Con-tuilet i n-deilb dá géise co timchellsat a l-loch fo thrí conná bed ní bad meth n-enech dó-som. To-comlat ass i n-deilb dá én find co m-batar ocin Bruig Maicc in Óicc, ocus chechnatar cocetal cíuil co corastar inna dóini i súan trí láa ocus teora n-aidche. Anais laiss ind ingen íar sin.

Is de sin ro boí cairdes in Maicc Óic ocus Ailella ocus Medbae. Is de sin do-cuaid Óengus, tricha cét, co Ailill ocus Meidb do tháin inna m-bó a Cúailnge.

Conid 'De Aislingiu Óenguso maicc in Dagdai' ainm in scéuil sin isin Táin Bó Cúailnge.

- Shaw, F., (1934) Aislinge Óenguso

Oengus's Dream

Óengus was sleeping when he saw a desirable thing.
He saw something, the girl appearing to him while he
was in bed, and she the most desirable in Ireland.
Óengus went to seize her hand to take her to him in his
bed. Then he saw nothing; he jumped up from surprise.
He did not know what she has flown from. He was there
until the next day. Not healthy was he because of his
thoughts. He became sick from seeking the figure he
wanted to speak to. He did not take food in his mouth.
Moreover he saw her at night again. He saw her with a
timpán in her hand that was melodious. She played
music on it, to him, there with him until the next day.
However she was not with him before his first meal the
next day.

A full year thus while she visited about his bed there
so that he fell into a wasting sickness. He did not tell
anyone. He exhibited a wasting sickness later and there
was no one who knew what was with him. The healers
of Ireland gathered together. They did not know what

ailed him in the end. One was sent to Fíngen, healer of Conchobuir. He went towards him. He discovered in studying the man the sickness or wound on him and he discovered from the smoke or people going from the house there was a sickness there.

He addressed him apart.

"Indeed! Not active are your wanderings", said Fíngen, "You greatly love an absent beloved."

"You have judged my sickness on me", said Óengus.

"Falling in this unseemliness and greatly burdened you told no one", said Fíngen.

"It's truth to you[9]", said Óengus. "A beautiful maiden comes in the most desirable form in Ireland with an excellent appearance. A timpán in her hand, playing for me each night."

"No matter", said Fíngen, "Friendship for her was chosen to you; and let you send for the Boínn, your mother, to come to speak to you."

Someone was sent to her. Then came the Boínn.

"I am healing this man", said Fíngen, "to whom came a serious sickness".

---

[9] more colloquially "you are right"

Then they told the story to the Boínn.

"Now will his attending be by his mother", said Fíngen. "To him came a serious sickness; and you must travel around all Ireland, to see if you can obtain a maiden in the form seen by your son".

She did this until the end of a year. Nothing was found similar to her. After that Fíngen gathered them together.

"Nothing of help in this matter was found", said Boínn.

Fíngen spoke: "Send someone to the Daghda that he may help his son".

Someone was sent to the Daghda. Then came the aforementioned. "Why have I been called?'"

"To advise your son", said the Boínn. "It is better to you to help him. His manner is sorrowful. He is in a wasting sickness. He loves an absent love and no help has been reached".

"What use calling me?" said the Daghda. "Not greater my knowledge than yours".

"Greater certainly", said Fíngen. "You are the king of the sidhe[10] of Ireland; and let someone go from you to

Bodb, king of the sídhe of Muman, and the fame of his knowledge is in all Ireland".

Someone is sent. He welcomes them. "A nod to you[11]", said Bodb, "people of the Daghda".

"It is reached".

"What story with you?" said Bodb.

"This way with us: Óengus son of the Daghda in a wasting sickness for two years."

"How is this?" said Bodb.

"He saw a maiden in his sleep. We do not know in Ireland where is the maiden who he loved and saw. You are ordered by the Daghda to seek through Ireland a maiden in this form and this likeness."

"It will be searched", said Bodb, "and obtain for me a meeting at the end of a year to know the story".

He came after a year to the house of Bodb at Síd Al Femen.

"I made a circuit of all Ireland until I found the maiden at Loch Bél Dracon at Crottaib Cliach", said Bodb.

---

[10] *sidhe, later sí, ie fairy hills or fairies

[11] fo chen, seems to be an idiomatic expression, similar to mo chen, indicating a nod or bow, probably a welcome or greeting.

Someone was sent by them to the Daghda. They were welcomed by them. "News with you?" said the Daghda.

"Good news; the girl of this appearance that you sought is found. You have been summoned by Bodb. Bring out Óengus with us to see if he recognizes the maiden, when he sees her."

Óengus was carried in a chariot until he was at Síd Al Femen. A great feast was for them with the king at the head. He was welcomed. They were three days and three nights at the feast.

"Come out of it then", said Bodb, "to see if you recognize the maiden when you see her. Who you may recognize, no power have I to give her to you except you may see her only."

They came later until they were at the Loch. They saw there girls of marriageable age in three groups of fifty. They saw the maiden among them. The girls didn't reach only as far as her shoulders. A silver chain was between each two girls. A silver collar around her throat itself and a chain of gold shining on her. And there spoke Bodb: "Do you recognize the maiden yonder?"

"I recognize her certainly", said Óengus.

"I have no more power for you", said Bodb, "a great measure."

"That is no matter", said Óengus, "indeed; because it is she I saw; I have no power to bring her forth on the journey. Who is the maiden, oh Bodb?" said Óengus.

"I know certainly", said Bodb, "Caer Ibormeith, daughter of Ethail Anbuail from Sídhe Úamain in the district of Connacht".

Óengus and his people departed then to the region. He brought Bodb with him to speak to the Daghda and the Boínn at Bruig Maicc ind Óicc[12]. He told his story to them relating to them her form between shape and appearance as they had seen. And told her name and her father's name and her grandfather.

"Not fortunate to us", said the Daghda, "no control have we over your gloom."

"There is some good to you, oh Daghda", said Bodb. "Go to Ailill and Medb because the maiden is near them in their region."

The Daghda goes so he is in the land of Connacht, three twenties [60] of chariots in his company. Welcome

---

[12] Bruig Maicc ind Oicc, that is Newgrange

was given to them by the king and queen. They were a complete week drinking and feasting after that there with them.

"Why have you come?" said the king.

"There is a maiden in your country'", said the Daghda, "and my son has loved her, and been in a sickness. We have come hence to find out if you can give her to our son."

"Who?" said Ailill.

"The daughter of Ethail Anbuail."

"The power is not with us", said Ailill and Medb. "If we were able to we would obtain her for him."

"It is best to call the king of the sídhe to you", said the Dagda.

Ailill's steward goes to him. "A command to you from Ailill and Medb to go speak with them".

"I will not go", he says. "I will not give my daughter to the Dagda's son".

Notice was given to Ailill of this. "Not great his arrival; he knows why he was commanded"

"No matter", said Ailill, "He will go and the heads of his warriors will be brought with him."

Then arose Ailill's household and the people of the Daghda to go to the sídhe. They laid waste to the entire sídhe. They carried off three-twenties [60] of heads out of it and the king with them to Crúachan in captivity.

Afterward Ailill said to Ethal n-Anbuail: "Give your daughter to the Dagda's son."

"I have not the power", said he. "Her power is greater than mine."

"What greater power is with her?" said Ailill.

"Not hard; she is in the form of a bird each other year, in the second year in the form of a person."

"What year is she in the form of a bird?" said Ailill.

"She will not be betrayed by me", said her father.

"Your head from you", said Ailill, "Unless you tell us."

"I will no longer hold it with me", he said. "I will tell", he said; "you are diligently engaged in seeking her. The Samhain near this she will be in the form of a bird at Loch Bél Dracon, You will see special birds with her there and there will be three fifties (150) of swans about her; and I have feasting preparations with me for them."

"No matter to me then" said the Daghda, "because you know her essence you can fulfill this".

Later a friendship was made by them, that is Ailill and Ethal and the Daghda, and a surety was given to Ethal. The Daghda took his leave of them. The Daghda went to his house and related the story to his son. "Go around Samhain near to Loch Bél Dracon and you can call to her from the lake".

The Macc Óc went there by Loch Bél Dracon. He saw three fifties (150) of white birds on the lake with silver chains with golden ringlets on their heads. Óengus was in the form of a person by the edge of the lake. He called the maiden towards him "Come and speak to me, oh Chaer."

"Who calls to me?" said Caer.

"Óengus calls to you."

"Give your word on your reputation I may return back to the lake."

"I accept", said he.

She went towards him. He put two arms on her. They slept in the form of two swans and then surrounding the lake for three rounds so there was no failure of his honor to him. They went out in the form of two white birds until they were at Bruig Maicc in Óicc, and singing a song musically threw the people into a magical sleep for three days and three nights. The maiden abided with him there afterwards.

Then there was friendship between the Maicc Óic and Ailill and Medb. This is the explanation of Óengus's thirty hundred [3,000], with Ailill and Medb at the cattle raid of Cúailnge.

So that 'The Dream of Oengus son of the Daghda' is the name of this story in the Táin Bó Cúailnge

Tuath De Danand na Set soim

Ceithri cathracha i r-robadar Tuatha De Danand ic foglaim fheasa ocus druidechta, uair is fis ocus druidecht ocus diabaldanacht ro fhogain doib. it e-seo anmanna na cathrach .i. Failias, ocus Findias, ocus Goirias, ocus Murias. Ocus is a Failias tucad in Lia Fail, fil i Temraig, no gesed fo cech rig no gebead h-Erind . A Gorias tucad in claidheb bai ic Nuadaid. A Findias tucad sleg Loga. A Murias tucadcoire in Dagda.

Ceithri fiseda badar isna cathrachaib sin .i. Fessus bai h-i Failias, Esrus bai ic Gorias, Uscias bai a Findias, Semias bai a Murias. Is aco sin rofoglaimsed Tuatha De Danand fis ocus eolus. Sleg Loga, ni gebthea cath fria na fris inti a m-bid laim. Claidheb Nuadad, ni thernad neach ara n-dergad

[gap: extent: 2 characters]. O da berthea asa thindtig bodba, ni gebti fris inti a m-bid laim. Coiri in Dagda, ni teigead dam dimdach uad . An Lia Fail, fil i Temraig, ni labrad acht fa rig Erenn.

Ad-beraid, imorro, aroile do seanchaidib conid a n-dluim ciach tistais Tuatha De Danann i n-Erind. Ocus ni h-ead on, acht a longaib namorloinges tangadar, ocus ro loiscsed a longa uili iar tuidecht i n-Erind. Ocus is don dluim ciach bai dib side, at-dubradar aroile conid a n-dluim chiach tangadar. Ocus ni h-ead iar fir . Ar is iad so da fhochaind ara r' loiscsead a longa na r' fhagbaidis fine Fomra iad do fodail forro, ocus na ro thisad Lug do cosnum rigi fri Nuagaid. Conid doib do chan in seanchaid:

Tuath De Danand na set soim.

Cait a fuaradar fogloim?

Do rangadar suigecht slan

A n-druigecht , a n-diabaldan.

Iardanel find, faith co feib,

Mac Nemid, mac Agnomain ,

D'ar mac baeth Beothach bertach,

Ba loech leothach, lanfhertach.

Clanna Beothaich, — beoda a m-blad —

Rangadar sluag niath nertmar,

Iar snim is iar toirrsi truim,

Lin a loingsi co Lochluinn.

Ceithri cathracha,— clu cert —

Gabsad a rem co ronert.

Do curdis comlann co cas

Is d'foglaim a fireolas.

Failias ocus Goiriasglan,

Findias, Murias na morgal,

O maitea madmann amach,

Anmanna na n-ardchathrach.

Morfis ocus Erus ard,

Uscias is Semiath sirgarg,

Re n-garmand, — luag a leasa —

Anmann suad a s-sarfeasa .

Morfis fili a Failias fen,

Esrus a Gorias, germen,

Semiath a Murias, dind dias,

Uscias fili find Findias.

Ceithri h-aisceda leo anall,

D'uaislib Tuaithi De Danand:

Claideb, cloch, coiri cumal,

Sleag ri h-aidid ardcurad.

Lia Fail a Failias anall,

Gesed fo rigaib Erend.

Claideb lama Loga luidh

A Goirias, — roga rocruid.

A Findias tar fairrgi i fad

Tucad sleg nemneach Nuadat.

A Murias, main adbol oll,

Coiri in Dagda na n-ardglond.

Ri Nime, Ri na fer fand,

Ro-m-aince, Rig na rigrand,

Fear ca fuil fulang na fuath,

Ocus cumang na caemtuath.

Tuata.

Finit

- Hull, V., (1930) The Four jewels of the Tuatha Dé Danann. Zeitschrift für Celtische Philologie. vol 18

The Four Treasures of the Tuatha De Danann

The Tuatha De Danann were in four cities learning wisdom and Druidism, a time of learning and magic and diabolic arts on them. These were the names of the cities that is Failias, and Findias, and Goirias, and Murias. And out of Failias was brought the Lia Fail, taken to Tara, it cried out under every king who would take Ireland. Out of Gorias was brought the sword that was Nuada's. Out of Findias was brought the spear of Lugh. Out of Murias was brought the cauldron of the Dagda.

Four magicians there were in these cities that is Fessus was in Failias, Esrus was at Gorias, Uscias was in Findias, Semias was in Murias. The Tuatha De Danann learned from them wisdom and knowledge. The spear of Lugh, no battle could be sustained against whoever had it in his hand. The sword of Nuada, none escapes who is reddened by it. When taken from its attacking sheath, no conquest against whoever had it in his hand. The cauldron of the Dagda, no company went displeased from it. And the Lia Fail, in Tara, didn't speak but under a king of Ireland.

It's told, however, otherwise by historians that with gushes of mists went the Tuatha De Danann in Ireland. This was not so, but they came in many ships, and they burned all their ships after they came in Ireland. And from this gushing mist that rose from them, some said it was in mist they came. This was not true. These are the two reasons they burned their ships: the group of Fomorians would not find them and raid upon them, and Lug could not come opposing the kingship against Nuada. About them the historian said this:

Tuatha De Danann of the valuable treasures.

Where did they attain wisdom?

They drew in complete

Their Druidism, their diabolism.

Fair Iardanel, prophet of distinction,

Son of Nemed, son of Agnomain ,

His reckless son was active Beothach ,

who was a warrior of wounding, full of miracles.

Beothach's children, — fortunate their triumphs —

A host of capable warriors came,

After battle and after sad weariness,

With all their ships to Lochluinn.

Four cities,— deserved their fame —

Held primacy with great strength.

Always warriors in contention with sorrow

They were studying truth and knowledge.

Failias and pure Goirias,

Findias, Murias of great valour,

From which battles retreat outwards,

The names of the high cities.

Morfis and lofty Erus,

Uscias and Semiath always fierce,

To call them, — a source of value —

Their names, exceedingly wise,

Morfis was the poet of Failias itself,

Esrus out of Gorias, sharp-mouthed,

Semiath out of Murias, pleasant points,

Uscias the poet of fair Findias.

Four gifts with them from beyond,

The noble Tuatha De Danann:

Sword, stone, champion's cauldron,

King's spear violent death of great heroes.

Stone of Fal from Falias thither.

It cries out under kings of Ireland.

The sword moves to Lugh's hand

Out of Goirias, — a choice of wealth.

Out of Findias across the wide ocean

Was brought the deadly spear of Nuada.

Out of Murias, a vast, great treasure,

The Cauldron of the Dagda of heroic deeds.

King of heaven, King of helpless men,

May he protect me, King of kingly portions,

Man whose blood holds out against specters,

and strength of the noble people.

Tuatha.

The end.

In Gabal in Dagdai a Luirg

'Aed Abaid Essa Ruaid misi .i. dagdia druidechta
Tuath De Danann ocus in Ruad Rofhessa Eochaid
Ollathair mo tri hanmanna.'

Ocus is amlaid ro bai-sium ocus mac dó aigi fora
muin .i. Cermad Minbeoil, ocus adrochairsium a comrag
ocus a comlonn la Lug mac Cein la hairdri Erenn, dochuaidh in Dagda a muinighin a fhessa ocus a fhireolais
dus in ticfad anam ina mac, conad airi sin tucad mir ocus
tuis ocus lossa ma corp Cermada, ocus tuargaibsium
Cermatfora muin, ocus siris an doman fa Cermut, ocus
ro-siacht in doman mor soir.

Dorecmaingedar triar dósom ag imdecht na conairi
ocus na sligead ocus seoid a n-athar accu. Fiarfaigid in
Dagdai scela dib, ocus adubradar: 'Tri meic aenathar
ocus aenmathar sind, ocus seoid ar n-athar acainn aga
roind.'

'Cred agaib ?' bar in Dagdai.

'Lene lorc ocus lumann,' bar iadsan.

'Cred na buada fuilet forro sin?' bar in Dagdai.

'An lorg mór sa adchi,' ar se, 'cenn ailgen aqi ocus cenn ainbthean. Indara cend ag marbad na mbeo, ocus in cenn ele ag tathbeougud na marb.'

'Cred in lene ocus in lumann,' ar in Dagdai, 'ocus cred a mbuada?'

'Ante gabus uime in lumann, a roga crotha ocus delba denma, ocus a roga datha, gen bhes ulme. In lene tra, gach cness imma ragha, gan cess gan galor do denum di.'

'Taile in lorg am laimsea,' bar in Dagdai. Ocus tucsad ar iasacht in lorg do, ocus ro fhuirmesdarsum in lorg fo tri orro, ocus adrocradar a triur laiss, ocus ro thunius dar in cenn ailgen fora mac, ocus adracht na nertlainti ocus forurim Cermad a laim for a aigid ocus adracht ocus ro sill for in triur marb ro boi ina fhadnaisi.

'Cuich in triur marb sa filet at fiadnasi'? ar Cermad.

'Triar dorala damsa,' bar in Dagdai. 'ocus seoida n-athar acu ga comroind. Tucsadar iasacht dun lurig damsa, ocus ro marbusa iad dun dara cind, ocus do thathbheoaiges tussu dun cind ele.'

'Dursan in gnim sin,' an Cermad, 'in ni dia tainic mo bheougudsa gan a tathbeougudsum de.'

Fuirmis in Dagda forrosan in luirg, ocus adractadar na nertslainti an triar brathar.

'Nach fedabair bar marbad,' ar se, 'do bar luirg fesin?'

'Rofedamar,' ar siad, 'ocus ro imris baegal oruind.'

'Agamsa ata eolus bar luirgi,' an in Dagdai, 'ocus tugus bar tri hanmana daib, ocus tabraidsi iasacht na luirgi damsa co hErind.'

'Cred is chuir no is tennta duinn fris immar lurig do thorachtain duinn?'

'Grian ocus esga, muir ocus tir, acht co marbursa mo naimdi di ocus gu tathbeoaider mu chairdh' Ocus tuccad dosum iasacht na luirgi fan coma sin.

'Cindus roindfimid nada set fil againd ?' ar siat.

'Dias agaib fana sedaib aenfer gan ni, nogo ria tim chell chugi.'

Is ann sin tucsom in luirg sin i nErind ocus a mac, ocus ro niarb a naimdi di, ocus do thathbeoaig a chairdi, ocus do gabastair rigi nErenn a los na luirgi sin.

'Arai sin,' ar se. 'is mac dun Dagdai sin misi ocus gach a raibi do draidecht d' fhisidecht aigi, ata agamsa, ocus gach an fhogluim d'eolus ag an tsluag ut, ata agamsa sin, ocus racaid misi leatsu, a macaim, do thoigi in tsegaind7 ut guro impaidher a ranna ocus a faebra,' et reliqua.

Buach ingen Dairi Duind, ben Loga meic Eithlenn, is ma gnais dochuaidh Cermad mac in Dagdai, conad inn ro marbad Cermad la Lug.

Osbom, B., (1927). "How the Dagda Got His Magic Staff."

How the Dagda Got His Magic Staff

"I am Aed Abaid Essa Ruaid that is the good god of sorcery of the Tuatha De Danann and Ruad Rofhessa, Eochaid Ollathair are my three names[13]."

And thus he was and with one of his son's on his back that is Cermad Minbeoil[14], who had fallen in his combat and his battle with Lug son of Cein the high king of Ireland, the Dagda put his trust in his knowledge and his experience to see if he could bring the soul [back] in his son, so that around the body of Cermad where placed myrrh and frankincense and many herbs, and he took Cermad on his back, and he wandered the

---

[13] Dagda - good god

Ruad Rofhessa - Red of great knowledge

Eochaid Ollathair - horseman great-father, with oll - "great" meaning large or immense rather than exceptionally good

[14] "Minbeoil" means either small mouth or gentle mouth, depending on whether there is a fada over the i in min or not. I personally favor mín, gentle, docile, courteous, although self-restrained may be a bit odd as an epithet for a deity who slept with the high king's wife....

I find it interesting if it is minbeoil (small mouthed) that begbeoil, also meaning small mouthed, is one of the Morrigan's given names in the Tain Bo Regamna.

world with Cermad, and went towards the great world in the east.

He happened upon a trio together on account of journeying the path and the course with the treasures of their father with them. The Dagda asked their story, and they answered: "We are three sons of one father and one mother, and the treasures of our father are shared among us."

"What do you have?" said the Dagda.

"A shirt, staff and shield[15]," they said.

"What is the value that is on them?" said the Dagda.

"The great staff that you see," said one, "a gentle end here and a violent end. One end kills the living, and the other end restores to life the dead."

"What of the shirt and shield," said the Dagda, "and what are their values?'

"He that takes on himself the shield, his choice of shape and pure form, and his choice of coloring, while it

---

[15] in the original the three items alliterate "lene, lorg, ocus lomann" the first can be understood as a tunic or shirt, the second as a staff or stick, so going with shirt and staff we can keep a bit of the alliteration, but lomann is usually understood as cloak, however there are references in the Metrical Dindshenchas where it is translated as "shield", and I have gone with this translation as it then preserves the alliteration that the original Old Irish possessed.

is on him. The shirt then, every surface that's chosen, without debility without sickness happening to him who wears it."

"Give the staff to my hand," said the Dagda. and they gave the staff to him, and he arranged the staff on the three, and the trio fell by it, and then he put the gentle end on his son, and he bound the full strength and stability on Cermad; his hands to his face he rises, and he gazes on the dead trio there before him.

"Who are the three dead here before me?" said Cermad.

"Three who I met," said the Dagda. "and the treasures of their father where with them for dividing. They gave the loan of the staff to me, and I killed them with the second end, and restored you to life with the other end."

"Misfortune in doing that," said Cermad, "when that which restored me to life did not restore them to life as well."

The Dagda settled the staff on them, and the three brothers arose in strong health.

"Do you know you were dead," said he, "by your staff itself?"

"We know," said they, "and we dispute being slain off guard."

"I have knowledge of the staff," said the Dagda, "and have given you three your lives; give the loan of the staff to me to go to Ireland."

"What guarantees or trust for us that the staff will come to us?"

"Sun and moon, sea and land, only that it kills my enemies and brings to life my friends." And they gave to him the loan of the staff to remain with him with that concession.

"How shall we divide the treasures we have left?" they said.

"The treasures to remain with the two, one man without any, until his time is yielded to him."

Then he took the staff to Ireland and his son, and killed his enemies, and brought to life his friends, and he took the kingship of Ireland with the ends of that staff.

"On account of this," said he, "a son of the Dagda am I and each magic and wizardy that he had, I have, and every wisdom and knowledge from the host, I have, and I declare I will go with you, my boy, to houses of champions yonder sharp commanding portions and his sharp-blades," etc.,.

Buach daughter of Dairi Duind, wife of Lugh son of Eithlenn, had intercourse with Cermad son of the Dagda, and so Cermad was slain by Lug.

Miscellany

Holidays:

"Co brón trogein .i. lugnusad .i. taide fogamuir .i. is and dobroine trogain .i. talom fo toirtip. Trogan didiu ainm do talum."

- Meyer, K., (1910). Tochmarc Emire la Coinculaind, page 246

"Until Brón Trogain, that is, Lunasa, that is the beginning of autumn, that is, then the earth is sorrowing, that is, earth under fruit. Trogan is another name for earth."

~~~~~~

Belltaine .i. bil tene .i. tene ṡoinmech .i. dáthene dognítis druidhe tria thaircedlu ...móraib combertis na cethrai arthedmannaib cacha bliadna cusnaténdtibsin (MARG-L eictis na cethra etarru)

- Sanas Cormaic B102, (n.d.)

Bealtaine, meaning lucky fire or fire of abundance, a festival with two fires made by Druidic incantations...made for the young herds to receive blessing every year against illnesses [note - the herds need to be driven between the fires]

~~~~~~

Co ndénta a cluiche cacha bliadna ic Lugnasad .i. Coícthiges ria lugnasad & coicthiges iar lugnasad. Lugnasad .i. noasad Loga meic Eithnend ainm in chluiche.

-   Macalister, R., (1940). Lebor Gabala Erenn

With a festival every year at Lúnasa, that is 15 days before Lúnasa and 15 days after Lúnasa. Lúnasa, that is a death commemoration Lugh son of Eithne named the festival.

~~~~~~

Scél lemm dúib:
Dordaid dam,

Snigid gaim,

Ro-fáith sam;

Gáeth ard úar,

Ísel grían,

Gair a rith,

Ruirthech rían;

Ro-rúad rath

Ro-cleth cruth,

Ro-gab gnáth

Guigrann guth;

Ro-gab úacht

Etti én

Aigre re

É mo scél.

- Scéla Muicce Meic Dathó, (n.d.)

News for you

Hear the stag's cry

Snows of winter

Summer has gone

Wind high, cold,

Low the sun,

Short his track

Heavy sea

Deep-red ferns

Lost their shape

Wild goose cries

A usual cry

Takes hold the cold

On birds' wings

An ice time

This my news

~~~~~~

About the Gods:

10. Banba Fotla ocus Fea

Nemaind nar fodaind fathaig.

Donand mathair na ndea.

11. Badb is Macha mét indbais

Morrígan fotla felbais.

indlema ind ága ernmais.

ingena ána Ernmais.

- Macalister, R., (1940). Lebor Gabala Erenn

Banba, Fotla and Fea,

Nemain wise in poetry,

Danand mother of the Gods.

Badb and Macha rich in wealth

Morrigan powerful in sorcery

They encompass iron-death battles

the daughters of Ernmas.

~~~~~~

Maiche .i. bodb; ł isi in tres morrigan .i. maiche 7
bodb 7 morrigan, unde mesrad maiche .i. cenna daoine
iarna nairlech, ut dixit dub ruis. Garbæ adbae innon fil. i
lomrad fir maiche mes, i nagat laich liu i lles, i lluaiget
mna trogain tres.

- Irsan, Dublin, Trinity College, MS 1337 (H.3.18),
pp. 79c–83b

Macha, that is a crow, one of the three Morrigans,
that is Macha and Badb and Morrigan. Whence the
harvest of Macha, that is men's heads after the slaughter,
having said that, dark red [or 'who said that, Dub Ruis'].

Rough dwellings are over there. Where men sheer off Macha's crop, where warriors drive a multitude into pens, where the raven women cause battles.

~~~~~~

Machæ .i. badb. nó así an tres morrígan, unde mesrad Machæ .i. cendæ doine iarna n-airlech

- O'Mulconry's Glossary, (n.d.)

Macha, that is Badb or one of the three Morrigans, whence Macha's harvest that is people's heads after the slaughter.

~~~~~~

Macha .i. badhb, no feannóg. mol macha .i. cruinniughadh badhb, no feannóg

-    O'Clery's Glossary, (n.d.)

Macha, that is a crow or hooded crow, the heap[16] of Macha that is the collection[17] of crows or hooded crows.

---

[16] Mol – lump, rounded mass, heap
[17] Cruinniughadh – act of gathering collecting, hosting

H-i Ross Bodbo .i. na Morrighno, ar iss ed a ross-side Crich Roiss ocus iss i an bodb catha h-i ocus is fria id-beurur bee Neid .i. bandee in catæ, uair is inann be Neid ocus dia cathæ.

- Meyer, K., (1910). Tochmarc Emire

In the Wood of Badb, that is of the Morrigu, therefore her proven-wood the land of Ross, and she is the Battle-Crow and is also called the woman of Neit, that is Goddess of Battle, because Neit is also a God of Battle.

~~~~~~

Ré secht mbliadan Nuadat narsheng
Osin chuanairt chéibfind
Flathius ind fir chichmair chuilfind
Ria tiachtain in Hérind
I Maig Thuiredh, truim co trucha,
I torchair cuing in chatha,
Do cosnamaid bán in betha -

Ro lead a lám flatha.

- Macalister, R., (1940). Lebor Gabala Erenn

A space of seven years noble, graceful Nuada

Over a fair-haired warrior-pack

Ruled the greatly keen, fair-tressed man

Before going to Ireland

In Maige Tuired, heavy with doom,

By chance burden in the battle

From the bright defender of life -

Hacked off was his arm of sovereignty.

~~~~~~

…fobíth roboi Dien-cecht & a dí mac & a ingen .i. Ochttriuil & Airmedh & Miach, oc dicetul for an tibrait .i. Slaine a hainm. Focertdidis a n-athgoite indte immorro airlestis. Bótar bi notegdis esde. Bati slan a n-athgoite tre nert an dicetail na cethri lege robatar immon tibrait.

-    Grey, E., (1983). Cath Maige Tuired

…because of Dian Cecht and his two sons and his daughter, that is Ochtriuil and Airmed and Miach, nearby composing incantations over gushing water, that is the Slaine it's name. Throwing their severely wounded in it, indeed in the great vessel. They would be alive emerging out of it. Their severely wounded would be healthy through the strength of the chanting of the four healers who were around it.

~~~~~~

Dagda .i. dagh dé .i. día soinemhail ag na geintíbh é, ar do adhradháis Tuatha Dé Danann dó, ar bá día talmhan dóibh é ar mhét a chumachta.

- Stokes, W., (1897). Cóir Anmann

Dagda that is a good god that is an excellent god he was of the pagans; because the Tuatha De Danann adored/worshiped him, because he was a god of the world to them, because of the greatness of his power

~~~~~~

Manannán Mac Lir...inde Scoti et Britónes eum deum maris uocauerunt...

- Sanas Cormaic, (n.d.)

Manannán Mac Lir...the Irish and British called him the God of the sea.

~~~~~~

Brigit .i. banfile ingen in Dagdai. is eiside Brigit baneceas (ł be neicsi) .i. Brigit bandee noadradís filid. arba romor 7 baroán afri thgnam. is airesin ideo eam (deam) uocant poetarum hoc nomine cuius sorores erant Brigit be legis Brigit bé goibnechta .i. bandé .i. tri hingena in Dagdai insin. de quarum nominibus pene omnes Hibernenses dea Brigit uocabatur. Brigit din .i. breoaigit ł breoṡaigit.

- Sanas Cormaic B 129, (n.d.)

Brigit – a poet, daughter of the Dagda. This Brigit is a woman of poetry (female poet) and is Brigit the Goddess worshipped by poets because her protection was very great and well known. This is why she is called a Goddess by poets. Her sisters were Brigit the woman of law and Brigit the woman of smithcraft, Goddesses; they are three daughters of the Dagda. Almost all Irish Goddesses are called a Brigit. Brigit then from breoaigit or breoshaigit, 'fiery arrow'

Bibliography

Hull, V., (1930) The Four jewels of the Tuatha Dé Danann. Zeitschrift für Celtische Philologie. vol 18

- Irsan, Dublin, (n.d.) Trinity College, MS 1337 (H.3.18), http://www.asnc.cam.ac.uk/irishglossaries/

Lebar na Núachongbála, (n.d.)

Macalister, R., (1940). Lebor Gabala Erenn

Meyer, K., (1907) Archiv für Celtische Lexikographie

Meyer, K., (1910). Tochmarc Emire la Coinculaind

O'Clery's Glossary, (n.d.) http://www.asnc.cam.ac.uk/irishglossaries/

O'Mulconry's Glossary, (n.d.) http://www.asnc.cam.ac.uk/irishglossaries/

Osbom, B., (1927). "How the Dagda Got His Magic Staff."

Sanas Cormaic, (n.d.) http://www.asnc.cam.ac.uk/irishglossaries/

Scéla Muicce Meic Dathó, (n.d.)

Shaw, F., (1934) Aislinge Óenguso

Stokes, W., (1880). Irische Texte mit Übersetzugen und Wörterbuch

Stokes, W., (1894). The Prose Tales of the Rennes Dindshenchas

Stokes, W., (1897). Cóir Anmann

Made in the USA
Middletown, DE
08 August 2015